SEREN SHEEP

and her Little Lost Lambs

Eve Louise Davies

UNTIL EVERY CAGE IS EMPTY. —

Anon

Dedicated to all the animals of the world who have been (or will be) innocent victims of the unnecessary meat, dairy and egg industries.

Thirty per cent of profits from the sale of this book will be donated to the Lisa James Animal Sanctuary, UK.

Seren was a pretty sheep who lived with her mother and lots of other sheep in the grassy, green fields of Wales. Seren was looking forward to spring, as she was having a little baby lamb. When her baby came, she was overjoyed! She bounced from one end of the field to the other!

BOUNCE, BOUNCE, BOUNCY, BOUNCE!

Seren's little baby lamb was so much fun to watch, skipping and leaping around the field with all the other baby lambs.

Sadly, when summer passed, the farmer came and took all the little lambs away in his old, rusty truck.

Seren missed her baby
so much. She sobbed to
her mother and asked

why the farmer had taken her baby but Seren's mother didn't know either.

One day, Hywel Hedgehog shuffled over

to Seren and asked why she was crying. Seren explained about her cute, little, lost lamb. Hywel looked sad and stared down at the grass and then told Seren that the farmer sends the lambs to a place where they make the lambs into meat for people to eat.

Seren was so upset and never, ever, ever, ever wanted anymore little lambs but when spring came, Seren had not

one, but two tiny,
fluffy, little lambs!

She didn't want autumn
to come as she knew

what was going to happen. Autumn came and sure enough, the farmer arrived in his old, rusty truck and loaded up her little lambs.

The next spring came and Seren had just one little girl lamb. Seren called her Lilybet.

Summer passed. The farmer came in his truck but this time he loaded up ALL the sheep and little lambs! They all trembled with fear.

Seren and Lilybet hadn't a clue what was happening but then the farmer let them out into a great, big, new field, she had never seen before, with a sign on the fence saying, '*Animal Sanctuary*'. A lovely, friendly looking lady and kind looking man came over and stroked Seren and Lilybet. Seren heard the couple say that they would keep all the farmer's sheep happy and safe for the rest of their lives! Seren was so happy that once again she bounced from one end of the field to the other!

BOUNCE, BOUNCE,
BOUNCY, BOUNCE!

LOOKING LIKE A CLOUD

As fluffy as a cloud
White like the snow,
Always following one
another
Looking for grass to chew
and mow.

Our eyes so bright and
wide
Roaming fields speaking
"baa",
Bleating all the time

For our mothers can't be
far.

Wandering the hills in
flocks
Running from the chains,
Singing a song of "baa,
baa"
Escaping the free range.

Lambs so tiny and new
Save before it's too late,
All we want is to grow old
And not end up on a plate.

So, count the sheep at night
Jumping in your dreams,
Hopping over little fences
Just happy without the screams.

We are beings at heart
Keeping warm from our fleece,
Please don't take it away
Or I'll shout for Little Bo Peep.

Remember when you see
A sheep or a lamb,
All they want is to live
So please just understand.

A heart that beats inside
Beats for a reason,
Leave the heart to beat
happy
And cuddle instead of
eating.

As fluffy as a cloud
Just needing a little care,

We're just the same as your
pet
So please treat us as fair.

Paul Axtell

Printed in the UK

First Printing: Aug 2018
Eve Louise Publishing

ISBN- 9781983382550

Printed in Poland
by Amazon Fulfillment
Poland Sp. z o.o., Wrocław